A LETTER TO MY DAUGHTERS

A Letter to My Daughters

Remembering the Lost Dimension & the Texture of Life

THEODORE RICHARDS

WAYFARER BOOKS
ABIQUIU, NEW MEXICO

WAYFARER BOOKS

WWW.WAYFARERBOOKS.ORG

© 2019, 2025 TEXT BY THEODORE RICHARDS

Published in 2019 by Little Bound Books
Front Cover Image: by © Theodore Richards
Cover and Interior Designed Connor Wolfe
First Edition 978-1-947003-46-0
Published by Wayfarer Books 2025
Second Edition 978-1-965320-55-6

The author has tried to recreate events, locales, and conversations from his memories of them. In order to maintain their anonymity, in some instances, he has changed the names of individuals and places, he may have changed some identifying characteristics, and details such as physical properties, occupations and places of residence.

10 9 8 7 6 5 4 3 2 1

Wayfarer Books is committed to ecological stewardship. We greatly value the natural environment and invest in conservation.

―――

———

For the wild, and the child, in all of us.

Don't ask yourself what the world needs;
ask yourself what makes you come alive.
And then go do that. Because what the world needs
is people who have come alive.

—HOWARD THURMAN

The best way to know God is to love many things.

—VINCENT VAN GOGH

Memory is quite central for me. Part of it is that I like the
actual texture of writing through memory.

—KAZUO ISHIGURO

Nel suo profondo vidi che s'interna,
legato con amore in un volume,
ciò che per l'universo si squaderna.

I saw within its depth how
It conceives all things in a single volume bound by Love,
of which the universe is the scattered leaves.

—DANTE

Cosima, Calliope, and Vismaya,

I AM WRITING TO YOU FROM AN AIRPLANE, not remembering where I am or where I am going. If I land in Atlanta, I could still be in Chicago. It doesn't matter. I will find myself in a mall, like a mall anywhere, repeated stores, brands, scenes. Am I flying back from Africa, or is it Heathrow? Maybe it's Jamaica. Somehow, I cannot place myself.

Do you remember our trip to Jamaica? This was before Vismaya was born, and Calliope just a baby; but you, Cosima, should remember something about it. We went to a wedding at a resort, one of those all-inclusive places. Although we didn't stay at the resort, we spent a day there. It was an awful place, filled with American stores and with ATMs that dispense American dollars. Food notable only for its quantity and blandness—there is no jerk chicken at the resort in Jamaica, for it isn't clear if it's even Jamaica.

This is the American Dream Vacation: travel without depth; travel in the two-dimensional world; travel without really leaving.

I fly in planes from one monocultural outpost to the next, thinking back to the days when I used to travel the world. In those days, I once met an Australian in Samoa, on a flight from one Samoan island to the next, who spent his life installing ATMs in the developing world. He was an absurd and obscene man, going on about the prostitutes in Asia. ("You'll love the girls in Vietnam!" he kept saying. You might as well know now that this is how men talk.) He bought me beer and lobster in Apia, then we flew off to Wellington and Sydney, where he was disembarking and I was flying on to Vietnam. From airport to airport we flew, from airplane to airplane. This was my first stop on a journey that would take me around the world completely, a spherical, three-dimensional journey. A journey of dirt and blood. A journey of taste and bodily sensation. A journey of *texture*. It never occurred to me that this man's work was flattening the world, to remove its texture so that he could consume it, just as he, in his mind, removed the depth of the girls in Vietnam so he could consume them.

I am writing you because I want you to live in this world, to feel it in its fullness, its depth. I want you to fall in love with the world, flawed and sorrowful as it is. Your lives and the world as a whole—these are indistinguishable to me—depend on this.

Have you noticed that when we take a bus in Chicago people enter the bus but they aren't really there? Their presence is enhanced, mediated. Each person—except us—is attached to a small machine to which their attention is directed at all times. Occasionally someone looks up, gathering only enough from their surroundings to avoid bumping into things before returning their attention to the device in their hand. Have you noticed, when we take the bus downtown along Lake Michigan, its waves shimmering, that no one even looks at the lake? Everyone is on a screen.

This is unusual—a shared, democratic space, with the possibility of touching one another, of common ground. This is why we do it: I want you to see and touch people, the world.

You may notice also that I am different when I drive, separated from everyone with steel and glass. When I am in my car, the possibility of intimacy with another is lost.

If someone cuts me off I curse at the car. I do not perceive that there is someone behind the steel and glass. We are utterly disconnected. I would never do this on the bus, or walking, nor would they be so oblivious. The car symbolizes freedom, independence. Its structure is so real—steel and glass—and yet it is an illusion, or at least feels like one: the capacity to be alone. The car is the isolated, individual ego expressed in steel and glass.

When I walk the streets of the city, or drive its roads, I am often unable to locate my self. Spaces have been built up in the interest of profit. They are replicable spaces, sterile and climate-controlled. No one sweats; no one touches.

All this comes back to the screen, which tells you that you are a number, valued in your ability to purchase things, replicable things. And you, a human being, are valued only when reduced to number, replicable like the product. The less human you are, the more valued you are. The less human our culture, the more profitable.

The third dimension, depth, has been lost.

The screen reflects back to us a two-dimensional self that we have co-created with the mediators of culture. Complex equations have calculated us, deciphered us—we are no longer mysterious on the flat screen. The screen understands us perfectly. It can tell us what we will buy, calculate our preferences and patterns. We are simultaneously consumers and products.

I can touch the screen, but cannot feel the world.

The question is this: If I cannot locate my self in this new world we've designed, do I even know who I am?

Your salvation, our salvation, depends on your ability to re-discover this lost dimension. I fear for you and the world. What I can offer you in this fight you have on your hands seems insignificant in the face of a culture that would flatten the world out and steal your soul, in the face of a civilization that would poison your water and toxify your air. You are called upon to bring the world back to life. This is real work, hard work. I can offer you only memories, stories of the world before it lost its texture, its depth.

EARTH

Spain, Summer 1995

As a child, I used to dig in the space behind our garage. Ostensibly, my purpose was to build a fort. Sometimes I told people I was looking for buried treasure, or dinosaur bones, neither of which, unsurprisingly, did I find. But looking back, it was perhaps more about the digging than the finding. Perhaps more about the dirt itself than any treasures contained therein.

Fifteen or so years later I was digging again. In the summer between my junior and senior years of college, I came to the north of Spain to work on an archaeological dig. My days were spent brushing away dirt and pulling out scraps of rock and seashells, the garbage of our ancient ancestors.

I'd never been overseas before. A few road trips as a kid, a few flights around the States, but nothing like this. I arrived to meet my friend Matt—whom I really barely knew—in

Madrid with a ridiculously large and awkward bag. Matt called it "the body bag". It contained essentially everything I owned. So, in a sense, it really wasn't all that big at all. Anyway, I didn't yet know that traveling, real traveling, meant both bringing all of one's self along and, paradoxically, leaving so much behind.

This was to be the first summer of my manhood, the first summer I didn't come home to live with my parents. Matt and I wandered the streets of Madrid every night arguing politics congenially. He was from a working-class family of fisherman, I was from a multicultural urban milieu. He was bitter about the world and its changes, about the intellectual elitism of The University of Chicago. Bitter about the dying seas, which meant a dying life for a New England fisherman. Neither of us knew shit, to be fair.

We traveled north, to Cantabria, where the dig, *El Juyo*, was located. As time wore on, he soured on Spain and its charms. I grew to love it more and more. He resisted academia and its pretensions, too. "Typical academic bullshit" was one of his favorite phrases. When I started a brief affair with a girl from Providence, his hometown, our relationship soured, too. Something in him was cracking, some resistance to the new world he was entering, like Spain itself.

We were housed in a Jesuit seminary. This was old Spain, the Spain of Franco and Hemingway. We drank wine with each meal—often too much. We were American kids. In the evenings we'd sometimes go into Santander. While not as wild as Madrid, Santander, like all of Spain, was a celebration each night. The gates of the seminary closed early in the evening, so we had to remain out until dawn if we left. In Spain, this was no problem. The party, in old Spain, spilled over onto the streets when the bars closed and into the dawn.

1995 was before the world became flat. Spain was not Europeanized yet, was still something unique. Spain had taste and texture. One could go out into the streets with little cups of sangria and pass hash joints around and touch people, look at people. Find joy.

Day after day we entered the cave and dug in the dirt. We were trying to remember the world of our ancestors, lives lived within the womb of the Earth. 15,000 years ago, in the days before farming and cities and empires, human beings who were otherwise just like us came to live in this part of the world. They made their homes in the caves nestled near the coast, where abundant food could be found.

One day, the professor who ran the dig told us that we were going on a field trip to another cave nearby called Altamira. I'd never heard of it. We rode in our Land Rovers that day to this other cave, not especially interested or excited, to see some cave paintings, we were told. Altamira wasn't open to the public, and it was impressed upon us that this was a great privilege—I imagined that this professor must be jealous that his own cave lacked any evidence of such art, that he must have experienced being an archaeologist with a boring cave like I'd experienced being a basketball player who stopped growing at 5-7.

Paleolithic people lived in the openings of caves, not in their depths, but the paintings were done deep within. One had to enter the Earth in its black, moist depths to create such works. These were narrow, labyrinthine spaces. Those who'd excavated the cave had carved out walkways so we could stand up.

We navigated the tunnels until finally we reached the room. I'd seen little up to that point in my life—this had been my first journey overseas. But although later I'd see the pyramids and the Taj Mahal, The Great Wall and Great Zimbabwe, this tore open my soul like nothing before or after.

Above us were the animals, skillfully, mesmerizingly crafted. Predator and prey danced above us. In an age before electric lights, before agriculture, before screens, someone had crawled into the womb of the earth with fire and paint and had crafted a scene of the dance of predator and prey. The dance of life.

It is said that when Picasso saw Altamira he declared that everything since had been "decadence".

The cave paintings contain certain recurrent patterns and themes. The predator and the prey is one; the handprint is another.

Over the years I have reflected a great deal on what it is about Altamira that so impacted me. In truth, like a book I read in my youth and couldn't fully appreciate, I have re-experienced the cave as I have grown.

I realized, later, when I saw my own child pressing on the edge of her womb, that the handprints in the cave were those very same handprints—the handprints on the womb of the Earth. The human was giving birth. Emerging. And it was our capacity for art that was emerging, for creating our world in symbol and story.

We become human when we become artist.

This required depth. These ancient shamans could have chosen to write on the edge of the cave, on the Earth's surface, and perhaps others did. But on this day, they chose to enter the depths of the Earth, to encounter the black abyss of the cave and to be left with nothing but themselves. Like I did when I was a little boy, the ancient shamans got dirty.

In 1995, we entered the cave without cell phones. We were just there, looking. To experience the cave, we had to be awake. To create the masterpieces, our ancestors had to be awake. To live a poetic life, present to the texture of the world.

I'd entered the womb; birth was next.

RAIN

Mozambique, Summer 1998

It is late; the bar is closing. People drift away. I wander outside alone. The friends who'd come to see me in Mozambique have gone back to Zimbabwe. I am alone. It is raining. *Raining.* I haven't seen a drop of rain, or even a cloud, in months. It has been the dry season in the highlands where I've been living. I walk across the beach to my tent. *Shit.* It is filled with water. *Shit.* It is a leaky old tent that I've borrowed from a friend.

I try to sleep, but I am getting soaked. So I salvage what I can from my tent and go to the bathroom, the only shelter I can find.

There, in the rain, I spend the night in a bathroom in the poorest country in the world. It is there in its dim light, for the first time, that I begin to write.

In 1998 I was working for a Danish NGO in the highlands of eastern Zimbabwe. I came there because I was young and eager to do something I thought was meaningful. And, on a deeper level, because I wanted to fly as far away from the holes behind my garage as I could get. Africa seemed like the place to go. I wanted to learn from the African people, from the rhythm of African life. And I did! Each day I wandered out into the villages, across savannahs dotted with baobabs, plucking mangos as we went, to meet under trees with women who'd never been to school, women who'd been through wars and who'd raised families from the parched earth, and tried to teach them something. I was young and idealistic and stupid— but not so stupid that I couldn't see the absurdity of this. I was *their* teacher.

We imposed Western values and Danish efficiency with a colonial obliviousness: The White Man's Burden, cloaked in development aid. Living in a land with no clocks, with barely even electricity, without even the conception of linear time, we created a schedule of classes and expected the women to meet us at a time, say, 1:00. We'd wait for hours, my partner, Maxwell, a local who knew far more than his bosses, and I, and talked about our lives, our families, about America and Africa. Time, for the people of Manicaland, was not measured in numbers but in *activity*—it was, as Einstein understood it, inseparable from place, impossible to isolate. But we tried. You see, for the people of rural Zimbabwe, 1:00 came when the crops had been tended, when the children had been fed, the water had been fetched. When the people arrived, class started, not the other way around. We thought they were late—but we were always early.

I soured on the NGO after discovering that it was not only problematic in the ways that many NGOs are problematic—condescending to the people and dismissive of the traditional ways, economies, and wisdom; pushing people toward capitalist development at any cost—but also in unique and shocking ways: this NGO was corrupt and cult-like. So I left for Mozambique, which was only a short bus ride away.

In 1998, Mozambique had just emerged from decades of civil war. First there was independence from Portugal; then there was the war waged by America and South Africa to destabilize Mozambique because of its ties to the Soviet

Union and African liberation. Bridges were blown up, hospitals and schools destroyed. By the time it all ended with the end of the Cold War and Apartheid, Mozambique was the poorest country in the world. It seemed like the place to go for me: In 1998, I wanted to reach the edge of the world, not yet realizing that it was a sphere.

The border wasn't far from where I'd been living in Zimbabwe. Border control was chaotic and I had to bribe someone to get over. But I was determined and happy to spend the $20US to cross. I could easily have snuck through. There was little security—just a patch of mud and dirt. Men milled around, women carried children on their backs and supplies on their heads. I waited like the rest as everyone stared at me. A flatbed truck arrived and everyone got on. We passed through ragged streets and desperate towns. So many landmine victims, hopping. A man smiled at me and shared guavas. I was alive, really alive, as the wind blew in my long hair while I tossed guava skin into the bush. The flatbed let us off half way and I got off. From there I would take a proper bus to the coastal city of Beira.

When I arrived in Beira I was immediately accosted by the taxi drivers. One haggled, the other was the driver. I had been in Africa long enough to expect this. The haggler knew some English. "Where do you go?" he smiled. "Biques," I said, giving him the name of the beach bar I'd found in a guidebook where one could safely pitch a tent. "Ah yes," he answered. "I know this place. It is a good place."

The haggler pushed the car along while the driver started it. Finally the engine turned over and he jumped in. This really was a two-man job. They drove me from central Beira, the decrepit and beautiful Beira, African and Portuguese and colonial, falling apart but somehow unbreakable after so much war, through the high grass to the coast.

I spent my days walking the coast and swimming, listening to the surf. There were no tourists, really. An occasional aid worker or missionary showed up. Boys played soccer and men fished.

I'd wander into town on nameless streets. Old men sat in the square drinking espresso and *galao*. Fruit trees grew on the roofs of old hotels, now occupied by squatters. Indians sold spices. The port was filled with shipwrecks. I ate at a restaurant that was in an abandoned movie theater. It felt like no one had been there in years.

Days passed. Friends came and went. They'd found me, my friends from Zimbabwe, from a simple postcard I'd sent. Nothing more. In those days, we just found each other.

At night, there was the rhythm of the sea, pulsing like the breathing Earth, like perturbations on the quantum foam, like the water in my body. There is a stillness in the rhythm of the surf, something permanent about it. But its permanence isn't found in its changelessness; indeed, no two waves are the same. Each time a wave comes in, it contains universes of new molecules, new worlds, new stories.

On my last night in Mozambique, there was water. It came down through the tent and into my life, a gift I could never repay. It would find its way to the sea and become a part of the sea. I held out my hands in the darkness as raindrops fell. Many years later I would watch the blood drip into my hands as you, Vismaya, my third daughter, were born in my arms in another bathroom on the other side of the world. That night, in Mozambique, I would be born in water. I would begin to tell my story.

SKY

Pakistan/Iran, Winter 2000

In the bitter cold, I wander from the little shack into the town square. This is a border town. And like all border towns, it has its dangers. Yet this one is quiet. And dark. There are no lights. I have no way of knowing the time. Perhaps it is 4:00 in the morning, still hours before the border will open. My stomach lurches again. There is no bathroom, so I wander from the square into an open space in the desert. I shit in the desert on the ground. Diarrhea like water. I am miserable but feel a momentary relief. I wipe myself with some old tissue and pull up my pants. I find an old burlap sack and lie back onto it. From millions of miles away, the light of the stars enters my soul, lighting me. I am frozen and sick. But the stars! Diarrhea is a pathway to God.

After my encounter in Samoa with the ATM-installer, I had traveled to the Far East, down through Tibet to the subcontinent, and was now heading across Pakistan into Iran. I rode on a crowded bus through the desert, into the night. Although I was wearing some approximation of the local garb and my beard was long like all the other men— there were few women—I caught a few stares. There must have been something unmistakably foreign about me. For one, I was unarmed. Many of my fellow travelers carried AK-47s. Nor did I speak the local language. But perhaps there was something more, something essential about me that gave me away. This was no tourist route, surely not for an American.

I was riding through the barren and wild lands of western Pakistan, leaving the city of Quetta, toward the border of Iran. I'd spent weeks trying to get a visa in Lahore. The men at the consulate were not unfriendly; they simply shrugged their shoulders at me each time I came, explaining in broken English that I'd have to come back in a few days. They called me—not completely without affection I'd like to think—"the American."

Finally, it came. I'd gotten my visa, but I was told that I'd have to sign up for a "tour". Don't worry, they explained. As long as you buy the initial bus ticket, you won't have to actually participate in any tour. You just need to show that you have a plan. So I did. And finally, I made my way from Lahore to Quetta, where I'd be able to find a bus to the border.

Borders, I have found, can be most unpleasant places. Combining the inherent fascism of low-level bureaucracy and military with the chaos of the various scam artists and hangers-on who seek to dupe the newly arrived, they bring with them hassles of both the official and illicit type. The traveler is the enemy of both the law and lawless.

Borders are human constructs, of course. Animal migrations and weather patterns ignore them. And so do humans, largely. So they represent a constant, dynamic tension between movement and containment, freedom and regulation.

And at the same time, the border is something we all recognize. We cross borders, real and imagined, psychic and physical, throughout our lives.

As I rode into the desert, into the night, it felt like I was approaching something like the narrow hourglass of the great Asian continent. It wasn't something new that I'd find on the other side, but a new me.

It was an overnight bus. As sunset approached, the travelers eagerly peeked out of their windows. It was Ramadan, and everyone was eager for the sun to set so they could start eating. And smoking, as it turned out. Nearly everyone lit up when the sun set.

We passed camel caravans and only a few spare settlements. Mostly, this was a land without infrastructure. A single road through a barren landscape. As night fell, I started to feel sick.

Sickness is a part of travel, the part that one never really envisions when deciding to leave in the first place. I'd had far worse than this: altitude sickness in Tibet; malaria in Africa. But there are two particular problems that a traveler can have with diarrhea. The first is the awful feeling of bubbling and painful cramps; the second, the difficulty of finding a place to relieve oneself. A fourteen-hour bus ride is never comfortable. I'd done rides on the tops of buses in India and precarious journeys across the mountains of eastern Zimbabwe. But nothing quite compared to the overcrowded, smoke-filled bus across the desert with diarrhea.

Finally we stopped. There was nothing more than a shack at the side of the road from which tea was sold. Beyond that, there appeared to be nothing—nothing but darkness. There was no bathroom, so I wandered out into the desert to shit.

Feeling moderately better, I stumbled back to the bus, where I was greeted by the one person on the bus who stood out as much as me, a man dressed in the long robes of an Iranian cleric. He seemed far less wild than the others, more urbane.

"Do you speak English?" he asked.

"Yes."

"Where are you from?"

I told him I was from America. He smiled.

"Come," he said. "Come drink tea." And the cleric, my new friend, led me to drink tea by the side of the road.

We spoke briefly about America and Iran. I told him about my travels. He told me about his business. It turned out that this cleric was a smuggler. He advised me light-heartedly about the border.

We rode on through the darkness until finally, mercifully, we reached the border. It was still dark, and there were few lights. Everyone wandered off and I was left holding my bag and my belly in the dark. "The border does not open for another two hours," I heard someone say. It was my cleric/smuggler friend. "We have to wait". He pulled me into a shack where a group of men sat around a small fire. He gestured to me to sit down, which I did. He said a few words to the group; they nodded and shared some tea.

I sat dumbly, not comprehending a word that was said, and sipped my tea. Soon, the little group began to disperse, and so did I. I wandered out into an open space to shit again, then lay down on some burlap sacks. I looked up and my eyes met the heavens; millions of stars exploded into my eyes and my consciousness. It was the most star-filled night I'd ever seen: Orion poised to cartwheel across the Milky Way, receding murkily into the infinite depths of space, chasing the Pleiades "Glitter[ing] like a swarm of fire-flies tangled in a silver braid."[1]

At that moment, I remembered it was Christmas.

Being no Christian—at least no more of a Christian than anything else—I hadn't thought much about Christmas until that moment.

Christmas, you see, was rather low-key in the tribal areas of western Pakistan.

But as I encountered those stars, I felt something deeper for Christmas than anything I'd ever heard from any pulpit. I was alone and cold and sick, in a desert landscape. I saw now what the authors of that story had perceived: the coming of the light in the darkest of times, the birth of god in the humblest of places. Only in the dark can we see the stars.

The border was stress-free as my cleric/smuggler friend had promised. He waved to me as we parted ways on the other side. Neither of us—it was unclear to me who had faced a greater risk, the American or the smuggler—had any

---

1 From Lord Tennyson's "Locksley Hall"

troubles. I got on a bus heading toward the ancient city of Bam. The bus driver took my bag and scrawled something in Persian on it in marker. I never learned what it said.

Another bus. And more diarrhea. I tried not to make a scene, but the discomfort had turned to pain. After a few short moments, the bus stopped and a man in uniform boarded. I stood out differently from how I had in Baluchistan. The men here were mostly dressed in typical, plain Western clothes. Perhaps I stood out because I was trying too hard, with my long beard and Pakistani shawl. Whatever the reason, the soldier's eyes stopped when they met mine. He approached and said something in Farsi. I stared back blankly.

"Passport?" he asked.

I handed it over. He looked at it, then me. "You are American?" he asked. I said I was and tilted my head in affirmation, the way they did in this part of the world.

At these words from the soldier, the entire bus, which had previously been filled with activity and chatter, stopped and stared. The soldier turned around with my passport and left the bus. We waited. I was too physically uncomfortable to be bothered by the stares, which were more curious than unfriendly anyway.

A young guy sitting across from me asked, "American?"

I nodded.

The soldier returned with my passport. "Welcome to Iran," he said in a neutral tone.

The young guy who'd spoken to me offered a piece of orange.

As we rode slowly through the day and into the night, I exchanged a few words with him—he was trying to practice the little English he had. Only a few miles from Bam, the bus broke down. I'd experienced plenty of broken down buses. In India once I'd hitched a ride with a little Frenchman on my lap, one leg hanging out the side of the jeep as we rode through the dark countryside blaring our horn as cows and humans leapt out of the way. But being sick added another layer of unpleasantness to the situation. And Iran is noted for its cleanliness. I wasn't in the bush or the desert where I could just shit on the side of the road. The cramps were worsening.

But my orange-bearing friend must have noticed. He flagged a car down and negotiated a price to take me to a hotel. When I awoke in the morning, my cramps and diarrhea were gone. I was left with only the vision of the stars in the desert sky.

WIND

Wales, Spring 2001

I am utterly frozen, exhausted. I haven't been this cold since a miserable night in an Indian bus in the mountains, months ago. With only the shawl I'd bought in Pakistan and a cap from Tibet to keep me warm, I am badly underdressed to be riding a bike across the Welsh countryside on a March morning. I am so often badly underdressed, I think.

Down the hills I feel air, piercing me. Up the hills, I feel the muscles in my body. I am cold and alive. This is good. I can feel the wind, my skin, the chemical flow in my body.

I reach the jagged coastline in St. David's. The rhythm of the sea, not unlike the rhythm I'd heard in Mozambique, but rougher, rockier, more dangerous. I look to the west. I am heading home soon, and continuing my journey to the west. I will have circumnavigated the globe, a sphere.

From Iran, I'd crossed the Middle East before flying from Tel Aviv to Italy. I came to the home of my ancestors, Naples, and met my old friend Sergio on his island, Ischia. I'd met Sergio in Llasa, where I'd been recovering from altitude sickness and a related injury. We'd rented a car to travel from Lhasa to Katmandu.

Sergio was a traveler like none I'd ever met. He'd been everywhere—he'd sailed the South Seas, ridden a motorcycle across Africa. By the time I met him, he was among the oldest of the backpacker crowd, but also more adventurous than the typical backpacker, spurning the well-trod paths and places. He was no idealist. His only interest was in the adventure of the new. He hated the Chinese authorities, not because of the way they treated the Tibetans, but because of their threat to his own ability to move about freely. He'd attempted to leave Lhasa and was detained briefly by the Chinese police.

Sergio was interested in Tibet and Tibetans only as a context to move, to travel, to find adventure and novelty. He always found a way to play. At one point, during a tour of a monastery, he'd challenged the biggest monk he could find to an arm-wrestling match. When he won—the biggest monk wasn't all that big—he jumped on the top of a vat of yak butter tea, pulled his shirt off, and flexed. The monks loved it.

Ischia was empty when I arrived. A bustling tourist spot in the summer, Ischia in February was only occupied by locals. I rode a bike there, too, all around the island, all day. Rough and empty beaches, warm blue water. Spare countryside. Bread and cheese and fruit for lunch. At night I'd find Sergio's family and eat and drink—sauces made with tomatoes grown nearby and rabbits caught in the countryside; wines from vines next door—and listen to the rhythm of their lives. I could taste the dirt of Ischia in their foods, their voices.

I left Sergio and Ischia and went north, to Rome, where the rhythms were different. It was relatively empty there, too, and I wandered its streets and churches. Florence and its echoes of Dante. Venice and its labyrinthine streets. Paris and its cold, wide boulevards, its Jazz and Hip Hop-filled night reminding me of home.

Finally, I emerged from the Chunnel in London. I hated it. It felt, perhaps, too much like the place I'd left, too replicable, too familiar. Compared to the vibrant and chaotic cities I'd passed through in deserts and in the tropics, London seemed cold and lonely. Its real attractions were found in its colonial-imperial past and capitalist-imperial present: museums filled with looted treasures. The only good food came from its scorned immigrants from places conquered by the king's armies and Thatcher's industries. No one smiled. It rained every day, and each day was filled with thoughts of the journey home. It felt like the end.

After a week, I left London for another ancestral home — Wales. I took a train to Swansea, then a smaller train to the coast, to Fishguard. I'd chosen the place because it was near the ocean, because it had a hostel, and because it was close to the town of St Dogmaels where my great grandfather had come from. He'd been a preacher—self-taught—who'd come to the New World to preach to the Welsh coalminers in their native language. He'd reinvented himself there, calling himself "Teifion" after the Teifi River next to which he'd been born, his home. This act of reinvention was wholly American, but, paradoxically, wholly un-American— Americans are supposed to forget their past, their home places. He remembered. I came there to remember, too.

Fishguard was a little fishing town, devoid of tourists or even very many pedestrians. Dave was a young guy who ran the hostel; he and I got along well. I was the only guest. Each day I took to the road on a rented bike, up and down the Welsh hills, past flocks of sheep and little settlements. I went to St Dogmaels and found, next to the ruins of an abbey, the little house in which my ancestor had been born. I walked the banks of the Teifi.

I rode to St. David's, the smallest city in Wales, known only as a city because of its cathedral, the church of the patron saint of Wales. I visited the old church, then went to the sea. St. David's juts out into the western sea, the direction in which I had been traveling for the past year, the direction in which I will journey home. Land and sea encounter each other abruptly, sometimes violently, here. The lines drawn on the map—or seen from the climate controlled cabin of an airplane—bear no resemblance to this coastline. But it is the wind that mediates. It pierces you. It exposes the lie of the harsh line between land and sea. When the coastal wind hits you, you know that you are not entirely on land here, that there is something of the sea in you. You can taste it.

Out across the sea, on a clear day, you can see the gentle curvature of the Earth. It is here that I have reached the end of the journey around the Earth. A sphere. The sphere has a center—depth. Its surface has texture, like the pulsating waves, like the cliffs, like the bittercold winds.

On the sphere, there is no edge other than now.

Soon, I will return to the airplane. I will get on in Heathrow, a plane that has come from India, filled with Indian families on their way to Chicago. I will be almost fooled, for a moment, into thinking that this ride reminds me of India. It won't. It can't. I have come from India, too, but traveled overland to get to London. In the stale air of the plane, there will be no incense burning, no cow shit, no one selling chai in the corridors, no flies. I will ride back around the globe, the Earth, the spherical planet that is our only home, and could be riding from Cleveland to Buffalo.

The food on the plane has no taste, the final leg of the journey has no texture.

*　　*　　*

Our ancestors created culture and cosmos, and in between was wildness and chaos. We walked from these cosmos-islands knowing that the bulk of the world was darkness—but that is how we could see the stars.

When I traveled the world, I found ways to reconnect to the people I loved and left, found places where I could go on a screen and send an email or learn news from back home. But there were in-between spaces, too. This is the texture of the journey, the places where one confronts bumps in the road, encounters strange people and unfamiliar places. These are the dark places—not literally dark, but dark in that they require us to encounter the darkness in our selves. These are the places I want you to know. For our future, your future, depends on it.

I don't travel so often or so far any more—perhaps when you are all a bit bigger we will take to the road again, together. I see others take their children to resorts, like the Jamaican resort serving bland American food, but I cannot do it. Better to imagine a world from the backyard than to travel the world without texture. Without tasting it. Without imagination.

I offer you stories of my travels, of monkeys stealing my coconut from the back of a pickup; of hippos snorting at night beneath my house-on-stilts; of pyramids and temples; of places where they eat roaches or strange fruits. You love these stories, but the story of a journey around the planet is no fairy story, either. To travel the world of texture is to see a planet in peril. It is to see resources squandered and stolen. It is to see unimaginable poverty and suffering. It is to see a planet that is a sphere, an island—finite—running out of food to eat, water to drink, and air to breathe. All this seems incomprehensible from the view above in an airplane, or on a screen.

The Earth is, first and foremost, earth. It is not a Euclidian grid, not a screen, but *dirt*. At Altamira, I remembered how we entered the earth, its depth, its dirt, to become artists. I remembered how we are fully human when our hands get dirty. When we neglect the soils we neglect our souls, and imperil our selves.

Always remember to dig deeply.

The rains and the waterways of the Earth baptize us into existence. We emerge from water, born and re-born. Ours is a thirsty species: we are running out of water to drink. And we are thirsty for belonging, too. In Mozambique, I emerged into manhood from the ocean waters, from the rain, and from my own transition into a storyteller, a worldmaker. Birthing is bloody and messy and wet. When I caught you, Vismaya, in our bathroom, I learned this, and I am reminded of it every day.

Always remember to cry deeply.

Since the Enlightenment, we have fought against the darkness. We've turned it into something evil. The industrial revolution made ours a world in which there were no dark places. This has been extended in the Information Age in which there are no more unrecorded spaces. Everything is viewable. That which isn't seen isn't real, you will be told. But something is lost in this Faustian bargain. Light has texture, too—if it's all so bright, we are blinded. To see the beauty of the stars requires the darkness. Where we are raising you, in Chicago, the stars are scarcely visible. This fills me with sorrow. Indeed, in recording everything we do, in documenting our lives on social media, we have lost the dark times, the silent times, the times when we process the story in which to make it come alive. You cannot dream if you don't close your eyes.

Always remember to dream deeply.

You will know better what it means to feel this suffocation of living in a world that would deny your humanity. Urban America will teach you this. "I can't breathe!" is the cry of the oppressed masses who struggle for their lives, their humanity, in the face of killer cops. It could also be the cry of life on the planet as we toxify the very air we breathe. In Asia, I awoke each morning to the sound of locals who breathed in this toxic air coughing and hacking and spitting. My own phlegm was black when I spit. The winds of the Pembrokeshire coast showed me the texture of the air, reminded me that it is a thing to be cherished, not a void to be ignored and soiled. Where is the line between water and air, between night and day, between earth and sky? Wind mediates the Earth's surface, reminding us that even the air is not empty. Without air, you could not breathe. It is a thing, not an absence. It pierces your bones and gives you life.

Always remember to breathe deeply.

The journeys I took around the world were meaningful partly due to the specificity of place. Each person or place we love is cherished in their uniqueness, because we can see something in them brought forth in our relationship with them. The airplane and the mall, the quest to install ATMs in every village or to put everyone on a schedule—all these things remove the uniqueness of place, the texture of the world. This is how I love each of you—uniquely for the miracle of your existence as the singular you.

At the same time, circumnavigating the globe offered me a sense of wholeness, seamlessness, interconnectedness. Our planet is a sphere. While each perspective on it may be unique, it is also true that each perspective is equally central. Only in accessing our depth can we find the center. There is one Earth; she is unique. And you are called upon to fall in love with her.

Always remember to love deeply.

I can remember a time before we lost our depth, but more and more people cannot. In losing depth and mystery, we are losing our capacity to be child-like. Children teach us what makes us human. You are my teachers.

What made us human? This is both a philosophical and an evolutionary question. In some senses, life is seamless; just as it is difficult to draw a clear line between land and sea, it is also impossible to name the precise point that a species becomes itself. We do know that at some point an animal began to walk in groups in the African savannah doing things that had never been done before. This animal came out with a large head, a head so big that the infant required care and compassion and love. This was an animal without the sharp teeth of the lion, the speed of the hawk, or the strength of the hippo. It was an animal that had two great gifts: the human could come together in community and bring a world into being through symbol and story. This animal could sing and paint its visions inside the depths of the cave. And it could do so because this animal possessed a depth within itself. It could do so because it had a gift we are losing: the capacity to play and explore and be curious.

To understand the emergence of the human from an evolutionary perspective, one must understand the impossibility, the miraculousness, of our survival. Our capacities for communication, for imagination, and for community came from no extrinsic source; rather, they were brought forth in relationship, relations embedded in ecological processes. It is because of the texture of the world and its pain, its darkness, its depth, its sorrow, that something called the human soul was brought forth.

Do you remember the story of Hawk and Mouse that I used to tell you?

Mouse spent his days running from Hawk. Hawk was so fast, his vision so precise, that Mouse could sometimes barely get enough food for his family. Hawk required him to be constantly vigilant. The friends and family members who were Hawk's victims required Mouse to create stories of remembrance. He was tired in body and in spirit.

So Mouse prayed to the Great Mouse in the Sky. "Please, oh Great Mouse, please grant me this wish. I pray that you would make Hawk a little slower so that I could feed my family more easily and suffer less."

The Great Mouse in the Sky granted this wish. For a time, life was easier for Mouse. But soon he began to slow down. Soon, Hawk was giving him problems again. So he returned to the Great Mouse in the Sky and again asked for Hawk to slow down. And again the wish was granted.

For a time, things were easier. But again, in time, Mouse slowed down. He returned to the Great Mouse and again asked for the same thing and again it was granted.

This repeated itself until Hawk could no longer fly and mouse could barely run. Mouse had no more stories to tell.

Mouse was no longer Mouse.

One last time, he returned to the Great Mouse in the Sky and asked for one final wish to be granted: "Please, oh Great Mouse. Please make Hawk faster."

We are mouse. We think that we've made our lives better, but we've only made ourselves less human. Without a textured world, a world of struggle, we fall asleep. We lose our soul, our depth. We forget the old stories, the paintings that were once on the wall of the caves. These paintings are really found on the walls of the caves within our selves, a place we can no longer access.

I love how you greet me when I arrive at home after a long trip. I can't wait to see you. Vismaya, the youngest, the two-year-old, you will come first. You have the most energy, the least apprehension. Everything is a joy to you, a surprise. You run everywhere, dance constantly. Calliope, the three-year-old, you will be next. You will leap into my arms. Cosima, my nine-year-old, you will be last, more careful. But you will hug me, too. You will all be talking, laughing, crying. You will all have created something since I've been gone. You will all have a story to share.

You, my daughters, make worlds constantly. Each day is a world-building and world-destroying endeavor. The work of the child is play; and play is a process of making a world through story. Your power, the power of play, of childhood, is this imaginative capacity. It is indeed this capacity—the playfulness, the spirit of curiosity and adventure—that led our ancestors from the forest out onto the savannah. They made worlds too, and in doing so became human.

When I am at home, you, my children, give me the texture, the depth, I cannot find in the world. With you, I am not in the screen world, but living in three dimensions. The first thing a child does is *taste*. She puts things in her mouth to know the world, to learn its flavors, its sensation. This disgusts us, as we grow older. We forget how to taste the world, and in doing so forget how to be human.

The child not only tastes the world, but also makes it. Childhood and its play is the greatest adventure of our lives. Each moment, in childhood, is new—to re-experience this through them is a gift we cannot repay. And an adventure in adulthood—all my travels were surely this—is an attempt to recapture the playful adventure of childhood.

I try to remember how to be human. You remind me. But the world will conspire to steal your humanity, to deprive you of your depth, your mystery, your capacity to taste the world. This terrifies me as much as the burning forests and the rising seas—it is an apocalypse within. To teach you, I have to remember my own humanity.

I try, in the world we make each day, to be human, or to do things that will make us human: stay away from the screen; read books; get my hands dirty; make food; walk; carry things. But the world conspires against my humanity.

It is as if the world has become heavy, or we, the people, have grown weak. We need you to be strong: To carry things, in world that would rather us pay for the privilege of being carried, is the hardest work you'll ever do.

With Love,

Babbo

ABOUT THE AUTHOR

Theodore Richards is an educator, poet, and philosopher, and the founder of The Chicago Wisdom Project. His work is dedicated to re-imagining education and creating new narratives about our place in the world. He has received degrees from various institutions, including the University of Chicago and The California Institute of Integral Studies, but has learned just as much studying the martial art of Bagua; teaching in various settings and students; and as a traveler from the Far East to the Middle East, from southern Africa to the South Pacific. He is the author of eight books and numerous literary awards, including two Nautilus Book Awards and three Independent Publisher Awards. He lives on the south side of Chicago with his wife and three daughters.

WAYFARER

BASED IN THE ABIQUIU, NEW MEXICO

At Wayfarer Books we believe poetry is the language of the earth. We believe words—shaped like rivers through wild places—can change the shape of the world. We publish poets and writers and renegades who stand outside of mainstream culture—poets, essayists, and storytellers whose work might withstand the scrutiny of crows and coyotes, those who are cryptic and floral, the crepuscular, and the queer-at-heart. We are more than just a publisher but a community of writers. Our mission is to produce books that can serve as a compass and map to all wayfarers through wild terrain.

WAYFARERBOOKS.ORG